AMAZON ECHO:

Amazon Echo Guide!

SS Publishing

TABLE OF CONTENTS

INTRODUCTION

I want to thank you and congratulate you for purchasing the book, **"Amazon Echo: Newbie to Expert in 1 Hour or Less!"**

Technology has grown in leaps and bounds in the past few decades, from smart phones to smart tablets, from cloud computing to online shopping and shipping. So here we have yet another marvelous invention that stands testimony to the wonder of human ingenuity – *Alexa*! Giving Microsoft's Cortana, Google Now and the elite Apple's Siri a run for their money, Amazon introduces something new into the world of voice-command – the Amazon Echo, which they have fondly dubbed Alexa.

This book contains proven steps and strategies on how to help guide you through the process of getting your Amazon Echo up and running quickly and effectively. Not only are there details on how to work it properly, you also get information on the inner workings of the Echo so that you know your would-be personal assistant inside out!

If you are someone who considers yourself less than an expert when it comes to using technology based items – have no fear, our Echo guide is here! You will be using this hybrid gadget in your home in less than an hour with ease and confidence. The whole family will be able to enjoy and use the Echo to help them with a wide range of activities – from daily questions that they want answered to making sure you are on time for work with Alexa acting as your assistant! There are many rich features offered to you by the Amazon Echo, so here's hoping you can make full use of it!

Thanks again for downloading this book, I hope you enjoy it!

CHAPTER 1

WHY ECHO?

Before we get into why you should buy the Amazon Echo, or why it is the best product out there, let me first tell what the Amazon Echo is. Given the temporary working title of 'Project D' or 'Doppler', the scientists at Amazon's Silicon Valley and Cambridge labs have been hard at work to unveil Alexa to the world. Their very first revolution was the Kindle E-Reader; the Amazon Echo is the first product they have introduced since the Kindle in an attempt to diversify their business into more than just being an online retailer of goods. Different types of gadgets have been launched by Amazon in their quest to make their customers' lives easier by offering them the optimum level of service to make their days simpler and less stressful, and the Amazon Echo is another one of them.

Like Apple's Siri, Alexa is another of those wonderful voice-command softwares which works on a question-answer system and controls all the smart devices within your house. Alexa brings us one step closer to achieving that J.A.R.V.I.S level artificial intelligence that we keep striving for, and she is amazing!

If you are someone that is dealing with an assortment of questions throughout your day and you need answers right away, the Amazon Echo is the ultimate tool that can answer your questions as well as other perform other tasks such as playing music and being used as an advertisement tool. The Amazon Echo is an all in one product that can help you in different areas of your daily life – all you need to do is say the activating word, *'Alexa'* – or *'Amazon'* if you prefer – and you will receive the desired information you are requesting from Alexa.

If you are someone that is in need of a personal assistant then Alexa will be able to provide this for you. Alexa will help you in your day to day activities. I have expanded on how to use her in the most effective manner in the later chapters. For now, let me tell you why she is the best voice-command device out there.

Easy to Access

You will basically be led by the hand through the steps to manage your Echo that are easy to follow. All you need to do is set the settings for your personal preferences and you are ready to go. You will have your daily assistance handled through your Echo.

Exceptional Voice Quality

Did you know that Alexa can act as your own personal music therapist after a long, hard day? She has the most soothing voice out there and by that I mean that the Amazon Echo has an exceptional quality of voice! It is clear, it is loud and it is exactly what you need if you are playing some melodious music to enjoy your down time after a full day of running around and working hard. So you can look to your Amazon Echo as a source that can offer you some stress reduction after a difficult day at the office!

These features are what the Amazon Echo is all about – it is a way of trying to make your life less stressful by helping you out and by being your personal assistant.

Different Voice Recognition

Another wonderful and impressive feature of the Amazon Echo is that it can easily differentiate your voice among hundreds of others. Alexa is one smart cookie – she will pick out your voice in a crowd and retain it! The Echo can record your voice, then respond to it as and when it is needed.

Privacy Issues

Your Amazon Echo, when it is switched on, can record everything, even if you are whispering. Obviously, a number of people were not too fond of this feature. But what you forget is that it can only record if it's on! And you can delete your recordings to keep things private! There is a *'manage my device'* page on the user's profile along with a customer support team for deleting the unwanted recordings. We will get to those features in detail later, but you can trust Alexa to be a faithful keeper of your secrets!

Software's Updating

As with any device, it is only constant innovation that keeps it in the market. Apple has upgraded their iPhones all the way to iPhone6 and Amazon is doing no less! They are trying to launch new versions of the Echo in order to keep the users interested in this gadget. Not only have they been making changes in the structure, but they also have changed the activating word 'Alexa' to the word 'Simon'. The software is consistently updated, so that you can be sure of using the latest and the best out there!

Natural Voices

The system of natural language processing has been installed in the device. This is built on the principles of the Echo text speech engine. Having highly efficient processing systems means your voice will be invigilated properly. In simple terms, Alexa will understand what you want to tell her with ease! Most often, that is one of the biggest problems with voice command systems – which the input is more likely to be misunderstood. Alexa is miles ahead in this race, however; she can understand what you want from her with far less repetitions that any of her peers at Google or Microsoft!

Cloud Based Processing

All of the voices that surround you are captured in the Amazon web service. The Echo can hear the opening and closing of a door or if you are watching TV. Remember, it will not record if it is not turned on. The Cloud based processing is a special feature of the Amazon Echo which you are able to operate from manual operation through the remote control or via voice activation. Cloud computing is certainly the future – Alexa will back up all your data to the cloud without you even having to prompt her!

Hardware

There is heavy investment into the technology just to enable the user to enjoy using the device in a smooth manner. The main hardware that is installed into the Amazon Echo is the Texas Instruments DM3725 ARM Cortex-A8 processor along with the 256MB of LPDDR1 RAM, with a storage capacity up to 4 GB. This hardware helps to ensure that the voice quality of delivery takes place in a controlled manner when connected to Wi-Fi or a Bluetooth. As you can see, Alexa has a mean body to match her super smart mind, enabling her to be the best virtual assistant you would want!

CHAPTER 2

DESIGN AND SETUP

Before we get to the Echo itself, let me first tell you about how you can buy it. The Amazon Echo is a product to be purchased on invitation only, so if you have it – congratulations! You are one of the lucky ones! And if you don't have and want to become part of the Echo family – here is how you go about doing it.

First, log into the Amazon website – remember to sign up and activate your account if you do not already possess and Amazon user ID. Search for Amazon Echo, and click on it once the option appears. The link will take you to a page where you can put your name down in the queue and then click on the request invite button and fill in the details. Once you have signed up for the device, there will be an interim waiting period, following which you will be given notice that your device is available. Pay and have your own Amazon Echo shipped to you! And Amazon Prime Members can even buy the Echo at a nominal fee, though you will still have to request an invite to do so.

Once it has been shipped to you and you receive the package, do a quick check to make sure that all the items are there. The box should contain the following –

- The Amazon Echo

- Power adapter to be plugged in

- The Amazon Echo remote-control, which has an inbuilt

microphone, music playback and volume buttons

- The magnetic Amazon Echo remote-control holder, including an adhesive for sticking it onto non-magnetic surfaces

- AAA Batteries for the remote

- A Quick Start Guide

If you have all those items, then you are good to go! You can activate Alexa and start using your Echo! Before you do though, remember to register your product online under your Amazon ID so that you can avail all the services available to you.

It is good to understand the mechanism that makes the Amazon Echo a superior device. Let us have a quick look at the entire basics of the Amazon Echo before you start using it – this helps to make you ready and aware to become the expert in using it in the future. There are different technology blends that make up the components of the Amazon Echo, whether it is its voice recognition or storing data software.

How the Echo system works depends largely on the efficient components that are embedded into the gadget. That is why the Echo is oriented to react fast with instant results, therefore being highly effective.

Exterior

The Amazon Echo is made up of a metal designed in a cylindrical shape, helping to ensure that it will consume less space. It will only cover 3.27 inches on a table top. It is only 9.25 inches tall. It has a two inch tweeter and a two and half inch woofer for enjoying dense sounds and it also has a reflex port to leave impact on the lively concert.

Blue Light

On top of the Echo, along with the two buttons, you will find a thin, translucent banner running around the edge of the Echo's cylindrical perimeter. This banner has a light ring that flashes different colored lights. When you see the blue light start to glint in the Echo cylinder, that means it is on and ready to use. The ring will flash other colors too, and each of them have their own significance, which I will expand on in later chapters.

Microphones

The Amazon Echo is basically a voice command device that responds to you when you ask it questions. Obviously that makes the microphones an important feature of the Echo. The microphones are the vital component for recording the input given to the Echo device; there are seven of them that are present in the speaker, arranged in a circular pattern. Whenever you speak the activating word the Echo device, automatically it is turned on and starts working because the microphones pick it up.

Sensors

Sensors are used in helping with the action of the microphone. The sensors of the Echo are made up from beam forming technology that enables the Echo to hear voices from each corner regardless of the direction. This is the main component which is used to connect to the web services on your requests when you speak the specified keyword.

Remote

The remote control that goes hand-in-hand with the Echo allows you to control it quite well. Reminiscent of the Amazon Fire TV Remote, it is around 5 inches in length and has a rubberized grip. There is a microphone button near the top – press down on it and you can speak to Alexa without shouting at a high pitch. The remote also controls the volume and playback of anything you're using Alexa for through the Echo app on your phone. The best thing about the remote – it has a magnetic holster which allows you to lug it around the entire house and attach it to wherever you can without having to worry about carrying your Echo around!

So that is what your Echo looks like! I have told you about the hardware, now let us set it up so that you can get to using it!

Setting up the Device and the App

Even before you begin to set your Amazon Echo up for use, download your Echo app so that you can navigate the device properly. The app is absolutely essential if you want to use the Echo at all, so go on and download on it on any smart device! The app is compatible with the following systems –

- Android phones or tablets

- iOS phones and tablets

- Amazon Fire phones and tablets

After this, you can begin to set up your device, so that you can start using Alexa! Setting up your very own Amazon Echo and getting it to work is actually very easy. Plug it in first, after which you can activate your remote control by inserting the two AAA batteries

AMAZON ECHO

you would have received in the box. The second that the remote is activated, it will automatically pair itself up with the Echo – you don't have to do anything!

If you find that your remote is not pairing up with the device, then don't panic! Here is what you can do to make it work. As soon as the Echo app is accessible to you, go to *Settings,* choose your Amazon Echo and click on the *Pair Remote/Forget Remote* option. If this still does not work, and you experience difficulty in pairing the remote with its Echo, contact Amazon's customer support for help.

Your Echo has officially been set up now! Here are a couple of quick things to do before you start working. Your remote has already been paired, but you should give your Echo a name so that you can identify it and manage its settings. This feature is especially important when you choose to have more than one Amazon Echo devices at home. To do this, go to your *Settings* option in your Echo app on the left navigation panel. The unnamed Echo will appear as 'Your Amazon Echo' in the name field. Select it, delete the name and key in what you would like your Echo to be name. Once you have done that, select *Save Changes*, and return to your home screen. Your Echo now has its very own name! You can use this name change settings, to pair up over Bluetooth, etc. Remember, though, this name has no bearing on the wake word, which remains *Alexa* or *Amazon* – I will tell you more about the '*wake word*' later.

Now, we can get your Echo to start working! Let us connect it to the Wi-Fi network. To do that, first make sure that your Echo is plugged into a power outlet.

Keep in mind, the Echo only connects only to dual-band Wi-Fi. As a device meant to be used at home, it cannot connect to enterprise or ad-hoc networks.

Now open your Echo app and select the *Set up New Echo* option under your *Settings.* Pick up the device and on it, press down and hold the Action button for a few seconds. The circular light ring should turn orange in color – this means that your Echo and the mobile device are connecting. A list of all the Wi-Fi networks that are available will appear on the app. Pick out yours and click on the *Connect* option. Type in the password if there is one and your Echo will automatically connect to the Wi-Fi!

If you cannot find your network, pick *Add a Network* or *Rescan* to manually set it up. As soon as the network is connected, a confirmation message will pop on the app, and you can return to the home screen.

Remember how I mentioned that Alexa also works Cloud Computing? You can back up all your data on the Amazon Cloud and access it from any device on the go! And here is the best part about the Amazon Echo – you do not need to manually set up your Cloud! Unlike Apple and other cloud computing, Alexa automatically hooks up with the Cloud the moment your device is connected to the Wi-Fi network.

Also, you yourself can check to see if your Echo is connected to your Wi-Fi and by extension, your Cloud. Check the power LED that is located above the power cord – the light ring. If the light is a solid white color, then you are in the clear, plugged in as you are to both Wi-Fi and the Cloud. If the light is a solid orange color, it means that your Echo is not even connected to the Wi-Fi; if the orange color blinks, you are connected to your internet but not the Cloud. The light ring also turns other colors, the significance of which I shall explain later.

If you are having problems, these are things you can do to try and fix it. Go back to the Echo app and try to reconnect to your Wi-Fi. Make sure you have typed out your password correctly. Obviously, you also need to check and see if your internet router is working properly. Restarting the modem may help in that case, since the problem is not with the Echo. Sometimes, concrete material or walls can also block the signal, so move your Echo closer to the router.

You can try to unplug your Echo from its power outlet and then re-plug it and switch it on again. Go online and log into the Amazon website with your ID and check to see if you have registered your Echo. If you are not, do that first – this is absolutely important to make optimum use of your device. Once you are registered, go to *Manage your Content and Devices*, and click on the *Your Devices* option. Deregister your Echo and then log out of the Amazon account. Now try setting up the device again from the first and then log into your account again to re-register you Echo. It should start working now.

If you are still having problems, contact Amazon Help and Support to get your Echo up and running! This, too, you can access via the Echo app. Open it up, and select the *Help* option in the left navigation panel. Pick the *Amazon Echo User Guide* to check to see if there is anything else you can do. If there isn't, choose the *E-Mail/Call Customer Service* to contact Amazon Echo Support and they will help you get it set up properly!

The last activity in getting your Echo set up is to key a few personal details. You need to personalize your Echo and let Alexa get to know your preferences so that she can help you out better! The first of these is adding the location of your device. Once again, open up your Echo app, and go to *Settings* on the left navigation panel. From there, select *Device Location* and specify the zip code in which your Echo located. The Echo itself tries to set up the zip code by default, so if you find that it is already there, don't panic! People living outside the United States of America in particular, may have to key it in. either way, if it is already there, check to see if it's correct and then, press the *Save Changes* tab and exit. By doing this, you have already begun to personalize your Echo! You are letting Alexa know where you live so that she can tune into the local radio stations for you, and get you the local weather without any difficulty whatsoever!

The second in the list is to change your metric measurements according to your likes. To do that, once again go to your *Settings*. There, you can pick out what you want – for distances, you will need to choose between U.S and Metric measurements and for temperature, select either Fahrenheit or Celsius. This way, Alexa knows how to respond to you and you won't have to waste extra time in getting her to convert the units for you!

The next thing we are going to tackle is Amazon account settings. As I already said, you have to register your device with Amazon so that you can avail all the facilities and be connected to the Amazon ecosystem for updates and the like. Once you have registered, you can manage your account setting from the app or get Alexa to do it for you! The most important of these settings is the *Voice Purchasing* feature, which will allow you to get Alexa to do your shopping for you by just giving her a simple command.

To activate *Voice Purchasing*, go to your Echo app's *Settings*. Tap on the *Voice Purchasing* tab. There, switch on *Purchase by Voice* option. It will ask you to set a confirmation code which you have to give Alexa each time you ask her to make a purchase for you. Key in this four digit PIN, and then tap on the *Save Changes* option before returning to your home screen. Please remember – do *not* create a PIN you use for other accounts or services. You will be speaking this PIN out loud to Alexa, so anybody will be able to hear. The PIN only acts as a verification code for your purchase, so your billing information and credit card information are all safe.

This brings me to the next part of account set up – managing your 1-Click Settings. If you are a regular user of Amazon, you would know that 1-Click Ordering is automatically enabled when you enter your payment method and shipping address for the first time during your first order. Thus, when you click the Buy now with 1-Click option on the Amazon website, your order will be processed according to the information you have already given, which has been saved under your account. You can, of course, change the address under *Manage Addresses and 1-Click Settings.* Now, with the Amazon Echo, you don't even need to do the one click – set up your settings so that Alexa can do the shopping for you! Update your 1-Click settings to include the Echo, and Alexa will tap into your Amazon account settings to know the details when you ask her to buy something for you! This way, the only verification she will request from you is your *Voice Purchasing* PIN; your billing information is quite safe with Amazon!

Since Alexa is a home device, more than one person's account can be tied in to her! You can create a Household profile to give you access to joint to-do lists, music, and various other features. It gives you the option of making joint purchases or using your family's account across other Amazon accounts or devices. To get Alexa to include other Household accounts, go to your Echo app and select *Settings*. Under that, pick the *Household Profiles* option, which will allow you to *invite* a person to your Amazon Household. Ensure that he/she whom you are adding is present with you – as you follow the instructions that pop up on the app, they will need to key in their personal details and credentials in order to be added.

With that, the second adult has been added to your Household! Alexa will be able to access both accounts, though she will run only one at a time. You can ask her, "*Alexa, which account is this?*" and she will answer you. You can also tell her to switch accounts, by giving the command, "*Alexa, switch accounts.*" Shopping and to-do lists are common, though, any changes within these two will be noticeable in the app to members of the Household who has been registered to the Echo.

If you need to remove a person from your Household, return to your *Household Profiles* under *Settings*. Tap the *Manage your Amazon Household* tab, and select the *Remove* tab next to the individual you are deleting. If you are removing yourself, then tap your account and pick the *Leave* option. To finish the process, select the *Remove from Household* option before you return to the home screen.

Another quick reminder – by adding a second person to the Household, you are giving them access to use your credit card and billing information which has been registered in your account. This is why it is a good idea to activate your Voice Purchasing PIN – that way, Alexa will not buy anything without asking for the PIN and you can keep that to yourself if you are not comfortable with others using your cards to make purchases.

With all that done, your Echo is ready and rearing to go!

CHAPTER 3

USING THE ECHO

There have been many and continuous modifications occurring with the Amazon Echo – it is no longer bound to stay on your tabletop or counter but it is also in the form of a small pen! Many people from all around the world who are gadget lovers have stated that they wanted to see the Amazon Echo in a form that they could take off the counter top, making it a mobile item. There have been many similar devices that have been based on the principles of the Amazon Echo device. There is now the Echo pen and the Echo app – the latter of which is essential to the usage of the device. This just goes to show the proof of the impulsive revolution that is going on around the world. Now people can enjoy the pleasure of the Echo using their mobile phones, and even their pens.

Amazon Echo app in Tablets and Smart Phone

In setting up the device, we already saw why the app is so essential. You convert all your Echo's tasks to the smart phone. If, for example, you are saying *"Alexa, add one dozen eggs to the 'to do list'"* then this command will automatically be processed through your smart phone and your command will be responded to. You can also pair your Amazon Echo with your tab and enjoy its benefits here too. Obviously, this means that the first thing you have to do to start using your Echo is to download the app on one of your smart device – phone or tablet, whichever works for you.

Make sure you have all the specifications I mentioned earlier – you may have to update your operating systems to make it compatible with the app if you do not have the latest version required.

The app that you downloaded should look rather sparse. There will be very little displayed on the home screen. You will only be able to see the recent questions and commands you give Alexa. On the upper-left corner, you will see a small tab, which will give you all your options.

You have your to-do list, your shopping list, alarms and timers you want the Echo to keep an eye on, and then your music. You are given access to Amazon Prime Music, iTunes, iHeartRadio, TuneIn, Pandora and Spotify. While it will default to Amazon Prime Music, you can select what you want in your setup and make your playlists.

This may seem a bit tiring but the relief you will feel when you have paired your Echo with your smart phone will be tremendous. Once you have installed the device in your tablet or smart phone you will be easily able to wake the Echo and command it as your heart desires. You can also set your device through specific settings for your storing texts, information, and queries.

Perhaps the Amazon Echo is extending into so many new gadgets is because it wants you to become so obsessed with it that you won't leave home without it—and now because of its new gadgets you won't have to!

There are users of the Amazon echo that don't want to leave home without their echo pen in their pocket. Others are stating that they are getting so used to having their Amazon Echo as part of their daily lives, really enjoying the help that they get from it, with it helping to solve their problems, as well as enjoy the other benefits it offers them. It is a wonderful simple multitasking gadget that many people are getting very attached to.

Amazon Echo Pen

The Echo pen is something you can use to write down your notes and know that this piece of technology is there to assist you. With the amazing smart pen you are able to record the lectures, interviews and what not! It just means setting up smart pen - all you need to do is point and play now. You just start writing and hear the recordings to assist you in preparing for lectures and presentations. It is not too heavy it is slim and light and has upto 4 GB of storage – that is close to 800 hours of audio (at optimum audio quality). The other feature of the Amazons Echo Pen is that it is directly connected to the USB port and you do not have to attach it to build connectivity with the PC or laptop. The Amazon Echo Pen can be a great assistant for you during lectures or whether you are rushing to the office to present a project to your team.

Now that we have discussed the benefits of the app and looked into the Amazon Echo Pen too, let us how you can use to Echo to the best of its ability!

Using Voice Command to activate your Echo

The Amazon Echo does give you the option of switching it on with the button on its top and using the app to navigate the device. But to use it to its fullest capacity, remember, you have to use your voice! It is a voice command device, so go on and wake Alexa up with her name! The moment you call out her name, the light ring will flare up and your device is now ready to go!

'Alexa' is the Echo's *'wake word'*. When you say this word, the light ring should turn blue – this means that the Echo is processing your command. It begins to send an audio stream to the Amazon Web Services which will answer your queries. This audio stream will send even a portion of the second audio before the wake word. The audio stream will close once the Echo processes your request.

How can you know if your command has been processed or not? To confirm this, go to your Echo app and under your *Settings,* tap on the *Your Echo* option. Go to *Sound Settings*, where you can enable your '*wake up sound*'. This is a very short tone that will ping every time your wake word is recognized by your device. And if you want to know when the audio stream has ended, also enable the '*end of request sound'*. This is also a short tune that will play once the stream has ended and your request has been processed. With these tunes, you can be sure that your command to Alexa is being heeded.

What do you do if you have a family member named 'Alexa' who turns to you every time you call out for your Amazon Echo? You change the wake word, of course! Once again, go to your app on your mobile device, and select your Echo from under *Settings*. Tap on the *Wake Word* option, and there, choose '*Amazon*' instead of '*Alexa'*. The next time you call out *Amazon*, your Echo will light up and respond to all your questions!

Alexa's voice recognition is the best in the field – more than a few customers have reported that she sounds far less robotic than iPhone's Siri and that there are fewer chances of her misunderstanding what you say to her. Perhaps the best characteristic feature of the Amazon Echo's voice recognition program is that it only keeps improving as time goes on – it uses your voice recordings to make its results better! The processing of information by the Voice Services begins the moment your Echo turns on. This is to give you the best response time and accuracy. The Echo app also gives you the Voice Training option, with which you can easily set up and train Alexa to understand and answer you as you want her to.

Amazon also gives you an amazing, bookmark-sized list of all the things you can ask Alexa and expect her to answer with perfect accuracy and not a single mistake – your very own index, if you will! The topics are not limited to any one field; they are wide and varied, from world clock timings to weather forecasts, from music playlists to the latest Hollywood gossip.

And like I said before, Alexa is super smart – she does not need much time to catch up! You can simply as her, *"Alexa, what is the weather?"* and immediately, she will give you that day's forecast, without any delay.

Alexa also has her virtual fingers dipped into information pies like Wikipedia. This means that you have easy access to those databases – with *spoken information*, because, remember, Alexa is a speaker and a voice-command device. She can read out to you what you want, so that you can move around doing other work while listening to what she is saying!

The best part of the Echo is that it is essentially a device built to be helpful in the home environment, and not the office. It has no batteries, and has to remain plugged in constantly if you want it to work. Obviously, it means that you cannot lug it around with you to parties or picnics or any place without electricity. A number of customers found this to be a great obstacle in using the Echo – what you have to remember is that Alexa is a very purpose-specific device, unlike your other smart phone helpers out there. She is meant to be a homebody – she can do anything from wake you up in the morning to helping you with groceries, but she is meant to be used as an individual assistant at the home, where you can build your day in and around her. And for those who want to move the Echo around, you now even have the option of the Amazon Echo pen! While its features are lesser in number compared to the Echo itself, it serves as a good substitute for when you need it!

Voice Training with Alexa

As I mentioned, the Amazon Echo's voice recognition only keeps improving with time. Before you begin to use Alexa to her full capacity, if you can do some voice training with her, it will definitely help her recognize you better! She will be able to match your speech patterns better and in turn, respond to you without mistake.

Before you can get to the actual training itself, you need to keep a few things in mind. Make sure your Echo's microphones are switched on so they can pick up the sound of your voice. Do not use your remote – the whole point is to get Alexa to understand you even if your voice is muffled or far away and the remote defeats that purpose. To begin voice training, open your Echo app. On the left navigation panel, pick the *Voice Training* option, and then tap on the *Start* tab.

You will be asked to speak 25 different phases, so you will have to spend a few moments. Sit or stand where you would normally be when you speak to your Echo to get Alexa used to you. Also, speak normally – not too fast, not too slow. Talk to Alexa like you would talk to a friend to facilitate easy understanding.

If you want to repeat a phrase, tap the *Pause* tab, and then quickly select the *Repeat Phrase* option. Once you are done saying a single phrase, pick the *Next* tab to continue with the training. If you want to exit halfway through the session, once again select the *Pause* option and then choose the *End Session* tab to exit. Here is an advantage – even if you do not complete the session, Alexa will still process all the phrases you have said and use it to update her system so that she can help you better! Also, the Voice Training sessions are not recorded in the Dialog History as part of your interactions with the Echo, so you don't have to worry about sounding silly!

Dialog History

The Amazon Echo records all the conversations you have with it in order to improve its own accuracy and response time. This means, obviously, that there are transcripts of all your dialog with Alexa, and you can access these transcripts whenever you want to. Go to your *Settings* on the Echo app and tap the *Dialog History* tab. You will get a list of all your interactions with Alexa and there, you can choose the one you want to listen to. Press the *Play* icon near the transcript of the chosen conversation and the recording plays for you.

If you want to delete a particular conversation, select that one and then lightly jab the *Delete* tab. When you do this, you are not only deleting the interaction from the Echo, but also stop its stream to the Amazon Cloud. This means that the Home Screen Cards related to the interaction will vanish, along with all data backed up to the Cloud. If you want to simply remove the Home Screen Cards, and leave the data in the Cloud, go to your Home Screen and tap the *Remove* option next to the transcript to hide it from your view.

If you want to delete all you conversations with the Amazon Echo, go to *Settings* on your Echo app and pick out the *Manage your Content and Devices* icon. Select *Your Devices* under it, and then, from the devices that have been registered with your Amazon account, choose the Amazon Echo. When it opens, you will find the *Device Actions* drop down menu – open that and then tap the *Manage Voice Recordings* tab. Here you can choose to *Delete* all the conversations, which will remove everything that the Echo has recorded, both from memory and the Cloud.

Do keep in mind, though, that these recordings have been saved for a purpose and that is not to invade your privacy. The Echo works on a self-correcting principle; the recordings in your account are constantly monitored and analyzed to improve the perfection of Alexa's speech and response to you. When you delete these recordings, she has no fall-back database, and it may affect her performance when you the voice feature.

Your Echo's Light Ring Status

When I described the Echo to you, I mentioned the circular banner of translucent material that runs around the circular perimeter of the device – the one we called the light ring. We have already seen how this light ring is effective in identifying the status of your Wi-Fi and Cloud connection – here are some other ways in which the varying colors can help you with your Echo. These color codes are common to all Echos and are very specific. They will indicate the status of your Echo to you so that you will know the moment a problem crops up – what it is and how to solve it too.

To reiterate what I have already said, the light ring will flare up brightly with a solid, spinning cyan blue color when the Echo boots up. Before that, though, there is no light – this does not mean that your Echo is not switched on, only that it is waiting for your command to start up. The moment it hears the wake word and powers on, the light ring will turn blue.

When this solid blue colored light turns around and starts to point to your direction, it means that Alexa has begun to process your request. Ideally, the light will move in the direction from which your voice comes no matter where you are located – you will know this way if the Echo has picked up your command or not.

The orange color I have already told you about – the Wi-Fi and the Cloud. When the spinning orange light comes into play, Alexa is busy syncing to your Wi-Fi. But here is something else you should take note of – if the light turns violet, and begins to oscillate continuously; it means the Echo is having trouble connecting to the network. Follow the procedures mentioned above and try again to connect to your Wi-Fi.

On the Echo, there is a volume button. If move this button to the left or the right, you will be able to regulate the volume of the Echo to your liking. When you are doing this, the light ring will turn a solid white color, indicating volume adjustment.

Next to the volume button, you have the Microphone button. This also affects this ring of light. If you turn off this Microphone button, the band will emit a solid red light, indicating that it is off and it cannot pick up your voice via the perforations. You will have to press the button again to turn it on if you want Alexa to listen to what you command.

Operating the Echo using the Remote-Control

If you are not comfortable using the voice commands, or you cannot speak directly to Alexa for some reason, you can use the remote control as an alternative! As we have already discussed, you will need to pair up your remote to the Echo to use it properly. Remember, only *one* Echo can be paired up with *one* remote control at any given time. If you have lost yours and ordered a replacement, you will first have to get the new one paired up to the device.

Here is how to do that. Go and open up your Echo app, and go to *Settings*. Select the name of your Echo from there and choose the option *Pair Remote/Forget Remote*. Click on the *Forget* option to remove the previous remote and then pair up the new one so that you can begin using it.

To start using the Echo via the remote, first press and then hold down the button on top of it. Keep holding it down until you hear a small beeping sound. When this sound dings, you can be sure that the remote is ready to pick up your command. Continue to hold the button down as you speak your instruction into the remote itself. Remember, you do not need to use the wake word here because you are using a remote paired up to the Echo, which means that it will automatically accept your command without it! And here is another added advantage of using the remote – it will let you use your Echo even when the microphones are muted, or when the noise in the room is too noisy for Alexa to pick up individual voices and process normally via her usual microphones.

If you like, you can also try changing your remote start up beep sound. You could remove it too – once again, go to the *Sounds Menu* from your *Settings* on your Echo app, and take it off there. This is a bad idea though – the start up beep is how you know that your device is transmitting and receiving properly. Without it, you may continue to speak into your remote, but you will not know if it has transmitted or not and you may end up not realizing it if it does not work.

On the remote, other than the main menu button that you need to hold down to speak to Alexa, there are audio playback buttons. You can use these to pause, play, stop and adjust your volume to your liking. Using the remote essentially means that you are using Alexa without having to speak out your commands to her directly.

Bluetooth

Your Amazon Echo is a speaker, which means that you can get Alexa to play music for you whenever you want her to! Remember how we discussed her playing music therapist to you? Now you can get her to do that even if you do not want to access the music options available on the Echo app! The app gives you access to Amazon Prime Music, iHeartRadio, TuneIn, iTunes, Pandora and Spotify. But if you have another mobile device which has music you want your Echo to play, you can easily pair it up with Alexa over Bluetooth and get her to belt it out for you! Make sure your mobile device has Bluetooth capacity and then turn it on, ready to be paired to the Echo.

Now keep it within the Amazon Echo's range and command Alexa to get in sync with it. You do not even need to spell it out for her – instead, you can simply say, *"Alexa, pair."* Like I keep mentioning, Alexa is a smart companion; she knows what you want from her. Soon after you give her the command to pair over Bluetooth, she will start searching for the device you want her to sync with. When she finds it, she will respond to you and say, *"Ready to pair."*

Now this is when you go to your mobile device, open up your Bluetooth settings and the pick the pair options like you would with any other device. It may take a few seconds for your device to read the Echo, so be patient. If your device's attempt to pair with her has been successful, Alexa will tell you, *"Connected with Bluetooth."* You should get a confirmation message on the mobile handset as well.

With that, you have Alexa on Bluetooth with another mobile device! Go ahead and stream all the songs you want – get Alexa to blare out the music loud and lend life to you party! If you want, you can use the Echo app or the remote to connect Alexa to your device instead of speaking to her. On the app, go to the *Settings* and work your way to *Bluetooth Settings* from there. With the remote, simply speak into it to pass the command on to Alexa – either way, she will give you the same responses as though you spoke directly to her.

As soon as you are finished with all the songs you want to listen to, speak the command, *"Alexa/Amazon, disconnect."* You Echo will automatically shut off its Bluetooth and disconnect from your mobile device.

Do keep in mind though, that the Echo can read only music files from your mobile devices. If it is a smart phone, then things like phone calls and text messages cannot be accessed through Alexa's Bluetooth. Similarly, on a tablet, you cannot send or receive videos or documents or any other files over your Bluetooth connection with the Echo. You also cannot connect the Echo to other Bluetooth speakers and play music or send audio that way.

On the bright side, you can be sure that once your mobile devices have been paired up with Alexa, she will not forget them! You do not have to keep connecting via *Settings* over and over again. Just keep your Bluetooth switched on in your mobile device, and then command Alexa to pair with it, and she will do so without any hassle and allow you to play all the music you want!

Not only can Alexa read and play your music from another device, she also gives you control over it without having to touch your mobile device. Generally, when you connect to an external speaker via Bluetooth, you are going to have to use your device to navigate pausing, playing, resuming, increasing/decreasing volume and the like. Now, Alexa can do it for you!

Just get her to sync to your device. Pick out the track you want her to play, and then let her handle it! Use the following voice commands to keep your own hands from getting dirty –

- Pause
- Play
- Stop
- Next
- Previous
- Restart

This feature of the Amazon Echo has been fondly dubbed as the Hands-Free Voice Control for Paired Devices. Now, you can move around the house, doing all your chores and you won't even have to worry about getting your tablet/phone screens messed up due to dirty hands! Alexa will take care of it all, you just need to tell her what to do and she will do it for you!

Enjoy your Hands-Free Voice Control for Paired Devices! Quick reminder – this hands-free voice control feature is, unfortunately, not supported by the Mac OS X devices like the Macbook Air.

Amazon Echo's Music Services

Now apart from using Alexa to play music via Bluetooth, you can access many other music services! Like I already mentioned, the Echo gives you access for a wide variety of these, from iTunes to Spotify. Here is how you can use them to your heart's content. The first thing you need to do to listen to music from the supported music services is to make sure your Echo app is the latest version of it available online. Go to your app store on your mobile device, and search for 'Amazon Echo'. You will be able to see which version of the app you have; if there is an update, then tap the *Update* option to download it so that you can use the Echo to its full capacity. If you do not see an update, it means you have the latest version of the apps. Now, you can go onto enjoy all the music services Alexa offers!

The moment you register your Echo under your account, you gain access to all the music you have under your Amazon Music library. For those of you who do not have an Amazon Music Subscription, you should sign up right away, since it allows you access to a wide range of music genres and artists! And Amazon Prime members are able to enjoy millions of songs for free on Prime Music! If you are, however, a proud owner of your own Amazon Music Library, then the Echo works much the same – you can import upto two hundred and fifty songs from a computer to the music library for free, and you will have to get your Annual Amazon Music Subscription to increase that limit to two hundred and fifty thousand songs.

Since Alexa is already plugged into your account, all you have to do is tell her to play a particular song. Give her the command, *"Alexa, play the song (name),"* and she will scroll through your library immediately and play it for you. If, by any chance, the song is not in your library, then she will go search the Amazon Prime Music library or check with the samples in the Digital Music Store to see if it is available to you.

If you want to use the app instead of asking Alexa, then open it up and pick the *Your Amazon Music Library* option from the left navigation panel. You can either look for the song individually in the search field or you can browse your library by tapping on *Songs* tab. The same applies to choosing *Artists, Albums or Genres*, which you can ask Alexa to do as well.

Now if you want to access other music services like TuneIn or iHeartRadio, it is best to link your accounts in these services to your Echo. Open up your Echo app and under the *Settings* tab, choose *Music Services*. Here, you will find a list of all the music services the Amazon Echo offers. Pick the ones you want to link to your Echo and fill in the details – your accounts will be synced with the Echo and you will be allowed full access to them!

You can, in fact, play music on these accounts without linking them, but certain features – like creating a custom radio station in iHeart Radio – will not be available to you. To avail these facilities, you must link them to the Echo.

Once you have linked all your accounts to your Amazon Echo, you can go all out and play music from any of them on Alexa! You can build your own custom artist station on iHeartRadio or Pandora, you can tune in to any radio station on TuneIn or iHeartRadio and you can access podcasts and programs on them too!

You can even tell Alexa to like/dislike a song! Just give her the command, *"Alexa, thumbs up/down,"* when the song is playing and she will do it! Or you could also spell it out and say, *"Alexa, I like/don't like thins song,"* and she will do the same. From the app, select the *Now Playing* tab and choose the *Queue* option to display the current list. Choose the song you like or dislike and then pick the *thumbs up* or *thumbs down* icon to indicate your choice!

And as users of Pandora and the Prime Stations would know, you can even remove a track played too often out of rotation! Tell Alexa, "*Alexa, I am tired of this song,*" and she will automatically remove it from your selection. See, again, you do not even have to spell it out for her – she understands what you want without you having to say it! The app is equally smart – under the *Queue* from the *Now Playing* tab, you can choose the specific track and then tap the '*I'm tired of this track*' tab to remove it from your playlists.

You can ask Alexa to adjust the volume, to stop, pause, resume, restart, loop and shuffle the tracks as they play. She will even give you the pertinent information about the song, the artist, the album, when it was released and all other details – once again, just call out to her and ask her. Remember though, third party music services have restrictions, since those services do not allow for certain features. Looping the play list, for instance, is not supported in the TuneIn, Pandora, iHeartRadio, and Prime Stations. Similarly, going to the next or the previous song is also not supported by TuneIn; iHeartRadio and Pandora do not allow you to restart a track either.

Shopping for Music from Amazon

If you want to, you can get Alexa to buy the song you are currently listening to on the Amazon Echo radio stations! Or you could ask Alexa for it directly by the name of the song, artist or album. As I already mentioned above, Alexa will search through the samples in the Digital Store for you and if you like it, you can purchase the song without any difficulty, especially since Alexa will use you

1-Click Mode of payment!

To buy music, you must have your voice purchasing turned on. We already did that during the setup of the device, so you can jump to step two, which is to make sure you have your 1-Click Payment details all up to date. If that is also done, then simply tell your Echo, *"Alexa, shop for the song/artist/album (name),"* or if you want to buy the song currently playing on one of your Echo radio stations, tell Alexa as it is playing, *"Alexa, buy this (song/album),"* and she will do it for you! She will ask you for your Voice Purchasing PIN, as soon as provide which the song will be imported into your library and the money deducted from your account.

There are a few things to remember when you are purchasing music from Amazon Digital Store though. You need a U.S billing address, and your payment method must be issued by any of the U.S banks. If, by any chance, you are using an Amazon Gift Card in order to buy your music, then you have to be physically situated within the United States.

The Amazon Echo also does not – currently –support Complete This Album, pre-orders, or MP3 Cart feature. On the bright side, any music that you buy from the Amazon Digital Music Store is stored in the Amazon Music Library for free! They are not counted against a storage limit; your Echo can easily avail them for download or playback at any time.

And apart from all these facilities, you can even access your music purchases from a second account. Remember how we set up a Household account? If you are lacking in balance in your own account, you can use your family's money to buy it and then repay them later! Any of the many accounts registered in the Amazon Household can be used to buy the music; use the buy commands as mentioned previously, and wait for Alexa to confirm with you which account to use to make the purchase.If any wrong account is used, and you want to cancel the transaction, quickly command your Echo, "*Alexa, cancel,*" and the purchase will not happen. Switch accounts with another command – "*Alexa, switch accounts,*" – and then place the order to buy the music you want. Of course, the Voice Purchasing PIN must be known to all members so that the purchase can be made.

Quick Note – if you forget your Voice Purchasing PIN number, you do not have to panic! Select *Settings* in your Echo app, and under *Voice Purchasing*, you can re-enter a new confirmation code. *Save changes* and your PIN has been reset! Now you can buy whatever you want without hassle.

Other Connected Home Devices

As I have already told you, Alexa is your ultimate homebody companion, designed to make your life easier. And now, you can even connect other home devices to her which you can access via voice control! For instance, if you were cooking and your hands are busy and suddenly, the bulb of your light gives out and you need to switch on the backup light and you cannot leave because your hands are tied up and the oven is on a timer. What can you do? Never fear, Alexa is here! Just tell her to switch on the back up light and she will do it for you immediately!

At this instance, though, the number of these devices is limited to lighting and switches alone, providing by two companies in particular – Belkin and Philips. Don't you worry; the scientists are hard at work, trying to add other devices too, so that you can access everything in your home – from lighting to the air conditioning and thermostat – to Alexa to make your life easier!

Now, the first step in accessing these home devices is connecting them Alexa. To do that, go online and download the manufacturer's companion app on your mobile device. The app would have been put up the company your home device belongs to – set it up so that it can be connected to the Echo. Follow the app setup and you can do it without too much difficulty!

As soon as your app has been downloaded, connect your home device to the same Wi-Fi network as your Amazon Echo. Then, open up your Echo app and under the *Settings* tab, choose your Echo and press the *Update Wi-Fi* option to sync both the home device and Alexa to the same network.

Once you have synced both together, you need to add specific devices to the list so that Alexa will know which one you are referring to. Imagine, you want the kitchen light switched on, and the bathroom light comes on instead! To avoid such mishaps, you will to connect all devices to Alexa individually. Give her the instruction, *"Alexa/Amazon, discover my devices,"* and she will automatically search them out. If want to access it via the app, you can do that too. Go to *Settings*, and select *Connected Home Devices*, from where you will have to pick the *Add New Devices* option. Name your individual devices there and connect them to Alexa to give her unlimited access to them!

As soon as Alexa has discovered the device, she will tell you - *"Discovery is complete. In total, you have *** reachable home devices under this Echo."* if, for some reason, she is unable to find it, she will say, *"Discovery is complete. I couldn't find any devices."* This could mean that the device is not compatible or there could be some other problem. Contact Amazon Echo Customer Service for further help. If the device cannot be reached, it will appear as *Unreachable* in the app.

If it has been connected, that will also pop up on the app. If your device meets all the specifications and still the Echo is unable to connect to it, here are some quick-fixes that you can try to get it to sync. Go to the manufacturer's app that you downloaded previously, and check to see if the device has been set up properly. In case you have trouble setting it up, contact the company for help.

The next thing to do is to update the software for the device. Go to the app again, and check and see if there are any updates available – you want the latest version to be able to connect to the Amazon Echo. If there are new updates, then follow the instructions in the manufacturer's companion app to download them. Most often, these updates will include any fixes in the device's design or improve its Wi-Fi connectivity.

If your Echo detects the connected home device, but does not sync with it, it could be that it is unable to understand what you have named it as. Open up your *Devices* and check that the names there correspond to what you have named your devices on the manufacturer's companion app. Also, do not give names like 'bedr00m light' instead of 'bedroom light' – the double zeros in the middle will only confuse Alexa and she will not be able to respond to you. Name it properly and she will be quick to follow your commands!

As a last resort, restart both your Amazon Echo and the connected home device. Unplug Alexa and plug her back it, and follow the procedures accordingly for your home device to shut it down and then restart it. If the device is still not connecting, then call both

Amazon Echo Customer Service and the device's manufacturer for help.

And now, you can tell Alexa to turn on and off the lights, and she will do it! You will not have to lift a finger to flip the switch either way. And if you want all the light to go on and off and the same time, you can get that done too! The individual lights you have added, now you will have to make a group to access more than one at a time.

To do that, go to *Settings* on you Echo app and pick the *Connected Devices* option under it. Now create a Group there, and choose the individual home devices you'd like to access together. Give the group a specific name and viola! You can turn on, adjust brightness or turn off all the lights in your home without having to move a single muscle! Tell Alexa, and she will do it all for you!

Help and Feedback

If you have trouble with Echo, you can always contact the Amazon Echo Support for help! You can access them from the Echo app itself, as I mentioned during the Setup. Just open it up and go the *Help* option on the left navigation panel and you can either e-mail or call customer service with your need and they will get back to you as soon as possible!

If, for instance, you asked your Echo to do something and it did not do it, or did it incorrectly, you can let the Customer Service know so that they can figure out the problem. In this particular case, you can choose the exact interaction with the Echo you had a problem with on the app. At the lower corner of the card displaying the interaction, there will a *More* option. Pick on that and select *No* when it asks you if your Echo heard you correctly.

This kind of feedback is always welcome! If there is a very specific conversation with your Echo you want to bring to the notice of the Customer Support at Amazon, then go to your *Dialog History* under your *Settings* in the Echo app. Scroll through all the interactions you have had with Alexa and select the one voice recording you want to send. Next to it will be the *Send Feedback* option – pick that. Then choose the *Feedback Category* from the options given to you and type out all the details you want to share with Customer Service – any queries, any positives/negatives of the Echo you want fixed or changed, etc. once you are done, select the *Send E-mail* option, and exit. Customer Service will respond as soon as possible!

If you want to give just a general feedback, without any specifics, you can do that too. Select the *General Feedback* option in your app, pick the *Feedback Option* (if you are sure of the option, choose *Other*) and then type out what you want to tell them. You could give suggestions, or address any general issue with the Echo. For instance, you could talk about a specific feature you think the Echo should have. Or you could give your general response to the Echo itself and how much like/dislike it and why you feel that way. Any and all feedback will be accepted! Once you are done typing, send the mail!

CHAPTER 4

MAKING ALEXA YOUR HOME ASSISTANT

Most of us would love to have a device at home that could help us with a variety of tasks. It would be nice to have a device that we just had to ask for a weather report, or news updates, be our timer when we are cooking something etc. The Echo device is something that you will get attached to very quickly, and really enjoy having around your house and at the office.

With your Echo you will have some help in dealing with the daily things that crop up in your busy hectic life. Your Echo will be able to be your personal assistant in helping you organize your schedules, and provide some relaxing music when you need it. It will help you to build your weekly shopping list, adding things to it through the week as you request them. No more worry about forgetting to add something to your shopping list – you mention it to your Echo device right away and it will save it for you.

Here are some of those things you can get Alexa to manage for you –

To-Do List

It is great having your Echo device to have it add things to your different lists. If you need to add a meeting to your to-do list, you can tell your Echo device to add it to your to-do list for you. Your information will automatically be saved in the 'to do list' section. To access it, just choose this option in your left navigation panel. Or, you could just tell Alexa what you want by calling out her name and she will add, remove or change things on the list for you!

Place Timeline

If you want to keep records of your every move, then you need to select 'Home' in the navigation panel and then choose your desired settings. You can choose to either have the recorded conversations on or not, make sure to decide all of these important issues before starting the timeline's action.

Use Alarm and Timer

Alexa will be your perfect morning assistant – she can wake you up and then she can time you through your routine so that you are not late for work! To use the alarm facility on your Echo, simply give Alexa the command. Again, you don't even have to spell it out; just tell her, *"Alexa, wake me up at (time)"*, and she will set the alarm for that particular time!

Here is another benefit – you can mute the Echo, and Alexa still will not give up! The alarm will still ring at the set time, despite the light ring being red. Alexa is a determined assistant – she *will* get you to work on time! You can, of course, get her to snooze by saying, *"Alexa, snooze."* She will go silent for exactly nine minutes before blaring loudly to get you up and running again.

You do have to remember to reset the alarm yourself, since Alexa does not do it for you automatically. You can also set it up only twenty-four hours earlier. This may seem an inconvenience to you, but Alexa is much like a person – if you were to tell your friend a week in advance that they should wake you up at this time on this day, it is more than likely that they will not remember to do so. Since Alexa acts as a personal assistant, you will have to treat her that way; get her to set the alarm every night and she *will* wake you up, no matter what!

Alexa's Timer also works similarly. You can set it up to go off at the specific time only twenty-four hours earlier by giving the voice command. You can also give the number of hours instead of the specific time you want it to go off at – very useful for cooking or timing yourself when working out! Either way, Alexa will accept the command. She will also tell you how much time you have on the timer if you ask her. To pause the timer, though, you will have to open up the Amazon Echo app.

Echo Plays Music by Voice Activation

One of the great features of the Echo device is that it can play your music just by you giving it a voice activation command. You can choose from the navigation panel and select your favorite song – hearing your favorite tune should put you in a good mood, especially after a long and hard day!

CHAPTER 5

QUICK THINGS TO ASK ALEXA

You can do branding using your Echo device; you may look at it and think how can such a small cylinder do so much? You must ask simple and direct questions to your Echo device and they will be answered helping to solve your problems. Your Echo will offer you brands if for example you ask it *"Alexa, can you give me a suggestion for a gift for my brother?"* Alexa will give you an answer with choices of brands. This is the way that the user's problems can be solved along with promoting brands. Here are other important areas of Amazon Echo that are revealed when you know how to ask the right questions.

Asking for Low Budget Options

When you are making out your grocery list for the week or other essentials, you can also find out low budget prices by questioning the Amazon Echo with the desired price. Your Echo will display things that are under budget. Alexa will help you keep your income and expenses balanced!

Help for the Perplexed Mind

If you are having a day where you are feeling confused and uncertain on how to decide on certain matters, ask your Echo device for some proper direction and opinion. If, for example, you cannot decide what tie you are going to wear for your date that evening, then just command your Echo and you will get a satisfactory opinion. Alexa is your loyal companion – she will give you honest opinions and can even act as your very own psychiatrist!

Looking for a Book

If you are looking for a certain genre of book to read – such as a mystery novel - then give the information on what type of book you are seeking to your Echo device and you will get some suitable suggestions. Now you don't have to go through all the summaries for every book! You can get some help from your Echo device to find a suitable book that you are interested in. Alexa will narrow down as per your preferences – you just need to tell her what you want!

Asking about Food

You can get some help in finding some good foods or recipes for certain dishes that you are interested in. Just ask your Echo to look up a recipe that you are interested in, this will save you time in searching for yourself. Why not get your personal assistant to help you out even in the kitchen? You can use your Echo as a timer to set a cook time to as well. Alexa will help prevent you from burning another dinner and make sure the kids get well fed!

Getting an Opinion

If you want to get an opinion from your Echo device then all you have to do is place a keyword before the original command, and then ask your Echo for a recommendation. Take for example you wanted to hear some uplifting energetic songs, then just ask 'Alexa, *can you recommend some energetic songs?'* The outcome will be generated in your Echo system and the result will be you being provided with a couple of energetic songs.

Search for Sale

You can use the branding factor with Amazon Echo – it will gather all the important sales and deals on the essentials by merely asking it what you are looking for on sale, or say a keyword along with the shopping center you may be interested in shopping at. You can also ask your Echo what the latest trends and fashion guides are.

Narrow Your Restaurant List

You can ask your Echo what the best rated restaurants are in your area, ones that are having a suitable deals etc. This is another way of diverting customers to your brand.

The Amazon Echo offers users something new to add to their home, work, and school life. It has enough impressive features to add positive change in your home or professional life or both. The Amazon Echo is slowly becoming the center of attention due to its unbeatable qualities and specifications such as being able to problem solve.

If you are confused you have the option that you can ask the Amazon Echo to help you by making a 'to do list' for you to help you keep things together and organized. The Amazon Echo is easy and simple to manage making it friendly for most people to make use of including children.

No Longer Need Pen & Paper to make your weekly Shopping list

You no longer have to worry about sitting down with a pen and paper to write your weekly shopping list. Instead you can just speak and your Echo will prepare your list automatically. It can then be accessed on your smart phone when you are out shopping.

Get Echo to Turn on the Tunes

You may have times when you can't find your favorite tune on your smart phone's playlist; at times like these all you have to do is command Alexa to play your favorite music and you will have music in a few minutes. You can also select what volume you want your music played at as well as selecting a number of hit songs embedded in the library or playlist of your Echo.

Temperature & Atmosphere Teller

Your Echo will be able to provide you with instant temperature and atmosphere reports, letting you know if it is cloudy or sunny. It will offer you relevant information regarding the rising or lowering of thermostat along with the atmosphere.

Get Traffic information

Set your starting point as well as your destination on your Amazon Echo app. Alexa will then tell you the best route to take, and predict your expected time of arrival, along with giving you directions if you want them! Of course, you will have to take her along with you though – just plug her into your car and you are good to go!

Keep a Record of Your Conversations

If you would like to keep a record of your conversations then your Echo will record everything that you are saying. If you choose not to make use of this feature it can be turned off so not all of your conversations are recorded. The choice is totally yours - with the Echo you do have options. You can keep your secrets with your Alexa – she will keep them safe, while providing you with some fun music to listen to.

The Amazon Echo is a gadget with great potential that is able to help with many different things to make your life that much easier. It is constantly improving with new ways being added to it to help you in ways that are more suitable for different individuals. You can have the Echo pen if you are someone that perhaps has a lot of lectures that you go to it would be very helpful in recording your class lectures for you and it takes up no more space than a pen. So this size makes it perfect for easy and light transporting of it and it consumes next to no space.

CHAPTER 6

QUESTIONS ABOUT ECHO ANSWERED

I have taken you through the workings of the Amazon Echo from start to finish, but it is very possible that you still have questions that pop up when you are working it out for the first time. Below is a collection of questions or concerns that you may have about the Amazon Echo. Hopefully you will find the answers that you were hoping for. Some information may be repeated from the previous chapters; nevertheless, these FAQs will give you quick access to the information you want, instead of having to thumb through to the right section!

1. Can I turn off Purchasing Echo? Yes. You can go to *Settings/ Voice Purchasing* in your Echo app to turn off purchasing by voice. You can also set up a confirmation code that Echo will ask you to say out loud when you want to place an order.

2. How Does Purchasing Music Work on Echo? You can purchase digital music by asking Echo to purchase it. Echo will use your default payment settings to place your order. You can also require a speaking confirmation code, turning purchasing off, and see product details in your Echo App.

3. What Happens when I Delete Voice Recordings? When you choose to delete voice recordings, Echo will remove Home Screen Cards that are also related to those voice recordings. When you remove a Home Screen Card from your Echo App, the voice recordings related to that card will not be deleted. You can delete individual recordings by going to *History* in your *Settings* in the Amazon Echo App.

4. Can I Delete all of My Voice Recordings? Yes you can delete the Amazon Echo voice recordings. You may find that your experience with Echo is degraded by doing this. If you want to delete recordings associated with your account, then go to www. amazon.com/myx and select Amazon Echo, or contact customer service. While your deletion request is being processed you still may be able to play back the voice recordings that are being deleted. You can delete specific voice interactions by going to the *History* in *Settings* in the Amazon Echo App, then scrolling down for a specific entry then press delete button.

5. How Do I Delete Individual Voice Recordings? You can delete a specific voice interaction by going to *History* in *Settings* and scrolling or drilling down to the specific entry, and then tap the delete button.

6. Can I Review What I have asked My Echo? You can review your voice interactions with Echo by going to *History* in *Settings* in the Amazon Echo App. Your interactions are grouped by question or request. If you want to see more detail, then just tap a request. You can check to see or listen to what was sent to the Cloud for that entry by tapping the play icon. You may find that some of the interactions are incomplete these are when Echo does not understand you. You can help to improve this by providing feedback on inaccurate translations in *History Setting*.

7. Can I Turn Off the Echo Microphones? Yes you can turn off the microphone by pushing the microphone button at the top of the Amazon Echo to on or off. When you see the ring on the top of the Echo turn red, then the microphone is off. The Echo will not respond to the activate word until the microphone is turned back on. Even if the microphone is off, you can still make requests using your remote control for your Echo.

8. How Do I know that My Voice is being streamed to the Cloud by Echo? When you use the wake word for your Echo or press the action button on top of the Amazon Echo, or when you press and hold your Amazon Echo remote's talk button, the light ring around the top of your Amazon Echo should turn blue to indicate that your Amazon Echo is streaming audio to the Cloud to process your request or question. When you use the wake word for your Echo, the audio stream includes a fraction of a second of audio before the wake word, and closes once Echo has processed your question. Within *Sounds Settings* you can enable a *'wake up sound'* which is a short audible tone that plays after the wake word is recognized to indicate that your Echo is streaming audio. You could also place this at the end of the audio to let you know that the streaming has ended.

9. How Does Echo Recognize the Wake Word? Amazon Echo uses on-device keyword spotting to detect the wake word. When Echo detects the wake word it then streams audio to the Cloud, including a fraction of a second of audio before the wake word.

10. Will the Voices Services Improve with Time? Yes, Echo's voice services are designed to get better over time. For example, the voice services use your voice recordings to improve the results provided to you and improve our services. Also when you activate your Echo, the voice services begin processing some information, such as your music playlists, to improve response time and accuracy. You can help to improve the voice services by providing feedback within *History*, by using *Voice Training* in the Amazon Echo App.

11. *How Does the Amazon Echo Work?* You can either use the wake word, press the action button on top of the Amazon Echo, or press and hold your Echo remote's talk button, then ask Amazon Echo a question, such as *"what is the weather going to be like in Toronto today?"* You may choose to tell it an action like add bread to your shopping list. Your requests and questions will be processed in the Cloud so that you will get your answers or requests fulfilled by your Echo. Your Echo may exchange info with third parties such as your music titles, radio stations, and your zip code to fulfill your requests.

CONCLUSION

There is something about Alexa that is infinitely better than a cold, impersonal smart phone helper. It could be that her homely name – Alexa – is far more pleasant that Siri or Cortana which sound utterly professional. It could be that she is meant for a home environment more than a business one – she can convert kitchen measurements without hassle!

Whatever the reason, Alexa is, hands down, the best home assistant who can keep you company as you complete your household chores! She can play music for you as you vacuum, she can read out information for you when you are doing the dishes and she can buy things online when you are busy getting dressed! She is easy to use, easy to navigate and requires very little maintenance. The downside is that she is restricted to the Amazon ecosystem – but, for anyone who knows how to work his or her way through that, she is an absolute joy to use! Her voice recognition is incredible and the lack of batteries becomes irrelevant since she is a home device.

I hope this book gave you all the information you need to have your own Alexa up and running and helping you out through the day!

OTHER RECOMMENDATIONS

Below you'll find some of other popular books on Amazon and Kindle as well. Simply type the titles of these books on Amazon. com

FIRE STICK: AMAZON FIRE TV STICK USER GUIDE

RASPBERRY PI 2: RASPBERRY PI 2 USER GUIDE FOR OPERATING SYSTEM, PROGRAMMING, PROJECTS AND MORE!

GALAXY S6: GALAXY S6 UNOFFICIAL USER GUIDE

APPS: BEGINNER'S GUIDE FOR APP PROGRAMMING,
APP DEVELOPMENT, APP DESIGN

FREE BONUS

GET MY LATEST KINDLE E-BOOK "TOP 10 GADGETS OF 2015" FOR FREE

As a "Thank You" for downloading, and reading my book I would like to send you my latest E-book "Top 10 Gadgets of 2015" for F.R.E.E. This is no strings attached offer, just my gift to you for being a great customer.

Get Your **"Best 2015 Technology Guide"** for F.R.E.E

Get F.R.E.E "Best 2015 Technology Guide" by Clicking "Download Now!"

Download Now!

Get My Free E-Book Now!

No, thanks, I'll pass this opportunity. Take me to the site now...

Type the link to claim your free bonus!:
https://cracklifecode.leadpages.net/technology/

Made in the USA
San Bernardino, CA
25 August 2015